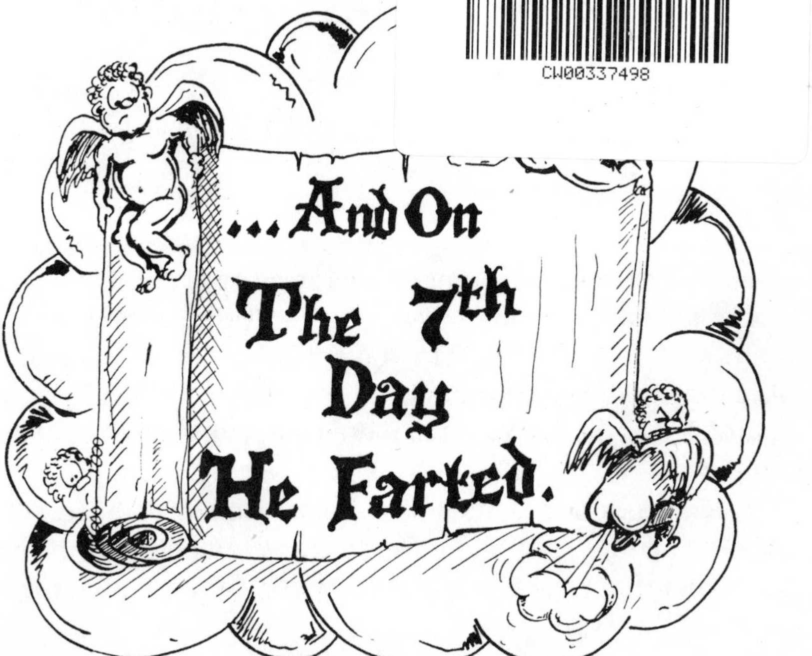
...And On
The 7th
Day
He Farted.

DINO-SORE-ARSES

In Prehistoric times, the world was ruled by gigantic lizards which were so large that they had two brains. Unfortunately, they needed a third to control the power of their equally gigantic bum-blasts.

Archeaologists have estimated that the average dinosaur's fart contained the same amount of energy as a small nuclear device. The combination of this awesome blarp power, and the lack of brain which was needed for good sphincter control, caused 70% of dinosaurs to explode under the power of their own farts. This, in turn, led to the extinction of these great pumping power houses.

One leading scientist believes that un-exploded dinosaurs are responsible for all the natural gas reserves found under the North Sea. Therefore, most people unsuspectingly use dinosaur farts to cook with today.

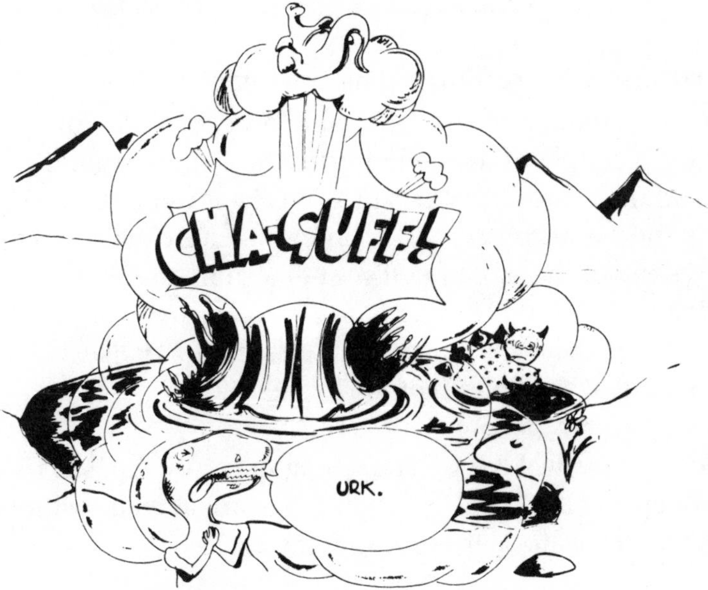
CHA-GUFF!
URK.

MESSY NESSIE

Fartosaurus Nessessitus was having a quiet bath one day in a small loch in Scotland when its mate suddenly exploded. Afraid to come out for a couple of days, the Fartosaurus discovered that it could control the power of its own farts by diving deep into the loch and using the water pressure to counter balance each rectal eruption. Being one of the more intelligent dinosaurs the Fartosaurus realised that it had found the secret to dinosaur survival and that it could never leave the loch. Fartosaurus Nessessitus or 'Nessie' for short, has stayed at the bottom of the loch ever since.

Visitors to Loch Ness often report sightings of a monster rising from the deep. This is a mistake, what they are actually witnessing is a small under-water parp breaking the surface.

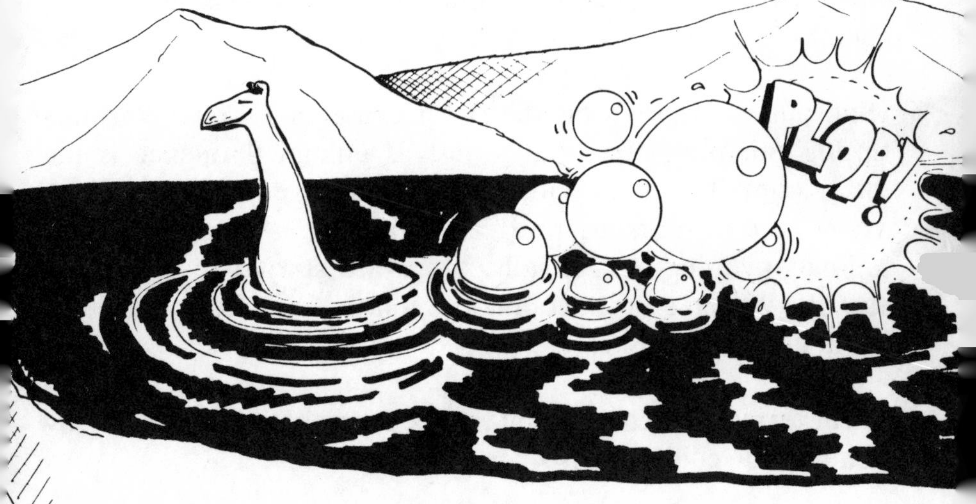
PLOP!

ICE AGE

After all the dinosaurs had died away the world was left without anything to generate the great volumes of gas that it had been used to.

Dinosaur fart had been the main cause of Global Warming throughout prehistoric times, just as animal flatulence is the main contributor to the present-day Greenhouse Effect. Without dinosaurs to produce bulk fart, and only smaller animals peeping occasionally, the world started to cool down rapidly. Within a quick couple of million years the Ice Age had set in good and proper.

Weatherman Micheal Fishfart reckons that this period saw some of the coldest farts since records began.

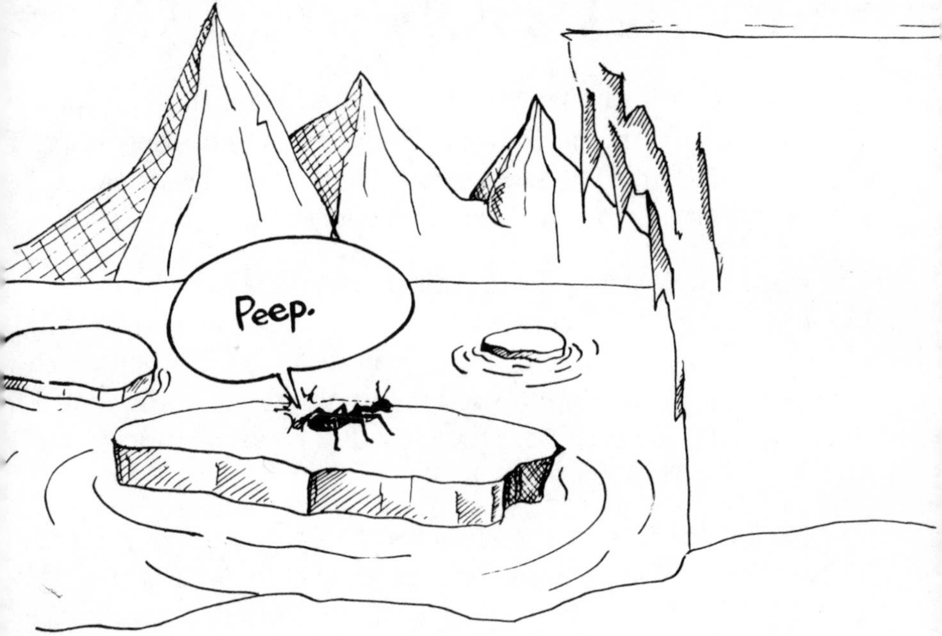
Peep.

═══ EVOLUTION OF MAN ═══

Out of the cold, however, came a glimmering fart of hope. One of the minor ape species discovered some dried plums which had fallen off a tree. After gorging on the prunes for several days the apes developed first degree chuffs.

The surprise explosions from their rear-ends caused the inquisitive apes to try and see what was going on. They could only manage this by standing on their hind legs. Once stood erect, the apes discovered that it eased the rumblings from their intestines. In fact, the straighter they stood, the easier it was to fart comfortably. And so man evolved.

Fossils of early man (Fartus Erectus) have recently been found. They show that the buttocks and nose have both decreased in size during evolution, presumably to further ease the passage of the fart and to decrease the perception of the foul smells produced.

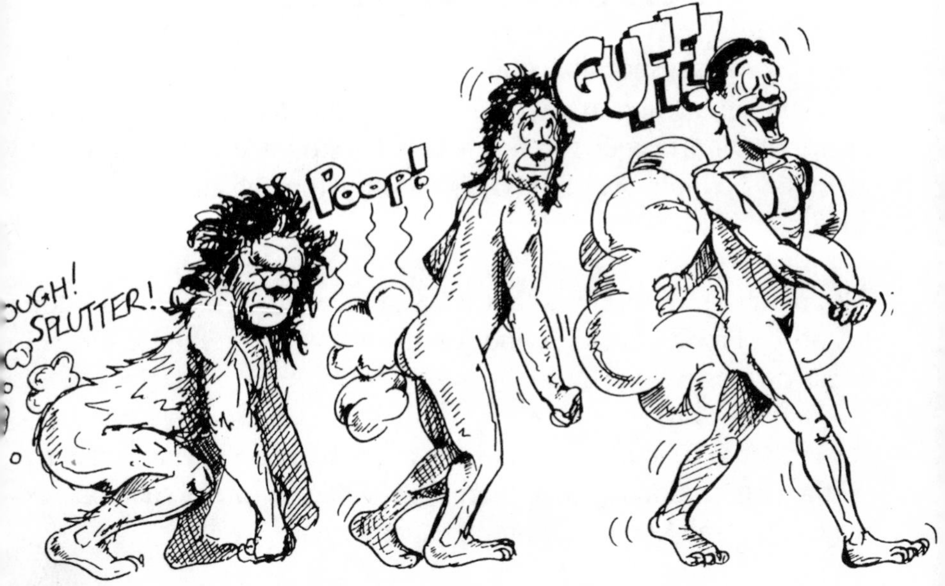
OUGH!
SPLUTTER!
POOP!
GUFF!

ADAM AND EVE

A snake was responsible for introducing an unsuspecting Adam to the damage farting can do. Adam was enticed to eat a slightly old apple which proceeded to ferment in his stomach. Not only did it give him a couple of sleepless nights with stomach ache, but it also gave him a good dose of the farts.

The result of all this, was that the snake left the Garden of Eden because of the awful smell, and Adam's eyes were opened to the evil of his own backside.

It remains uncertain if Eve had any of the bad apples which caused all the commotion in the garden. This could be one of the reasons why it still isn't known if women let rip or not.

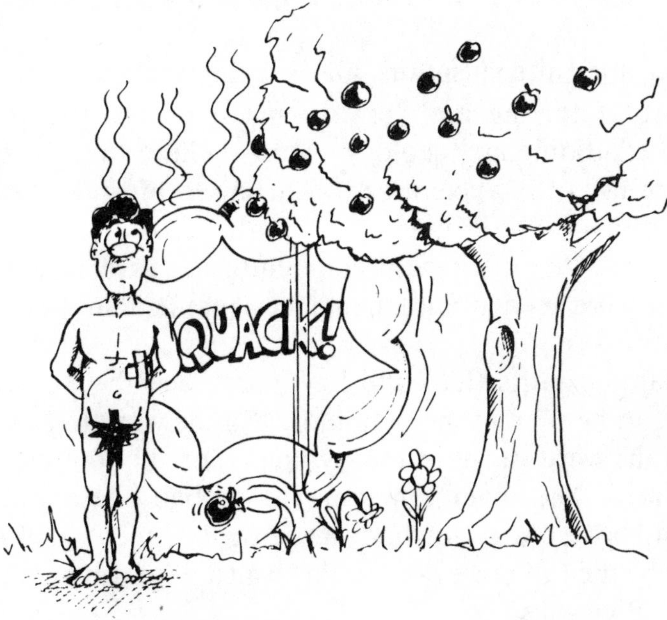
QUACK!

STONEHENGE

Many ancient civilisations all over the world soon discovered the art of farting and how to make use of the powers it unlocked. Some archaeology experts believe that the druids in Europe used the ancient art of farting to lift huge stones into the air when building monuments to the pagan god of trumping. One of these monuments has survived until today, and it can be seen at Stonehenge in Great Britain.

The same experts think the Egyptians used the ancient art of farting to help build the pyramids. All the worldly goods of the Pharaohs were put into the pyramids for the journey into the after life. The inner sanctum was probably reserved for the Pharaoh's best fart. Anybody entering the inner sanctum would be hit by the full power of the fart which is known as 'The Curse of The Pharaohs'

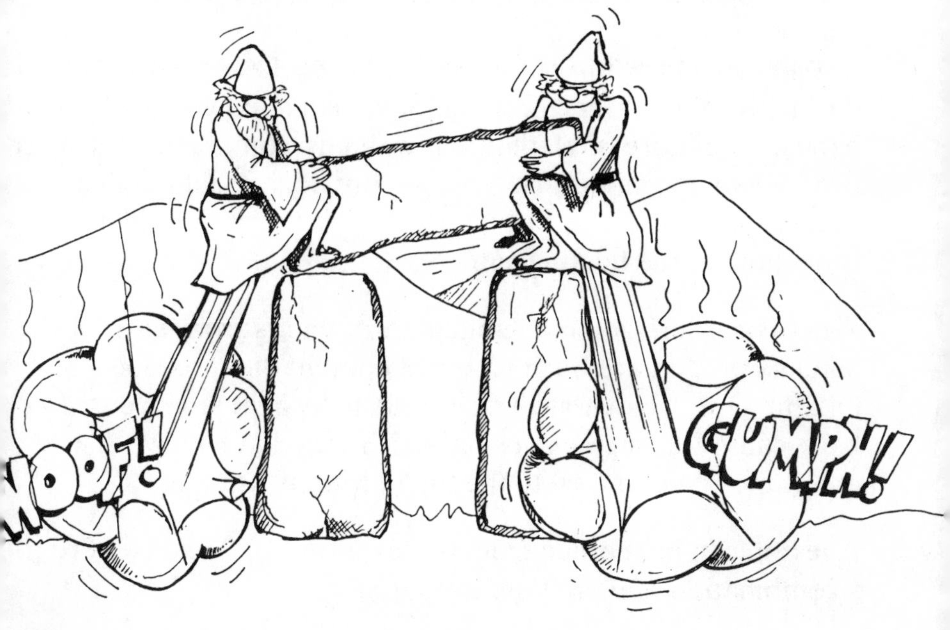
WOOF!
GUMPH!

THE GREAT FLOOD

Noah did the world a service by saving two of each animal during the great flood. What he didn't count on was their rectal habits. Folklore says that the animals continued to trump two-by-two for the entire voyage, but this could be debated because no one knows if the female of each species did, in fact, contribute to the floating guff.

What is certain, is the combination of chuffs from each of the animals would have been extremely potent and probably highly inflammable. Noah striking a match to light his oven could have caused a huge explosion which may have blown the ark out of the water and on to the top of Mount Ararat.

A lesson can be learned from this experience; do not set fire to a combination of more than two farts.

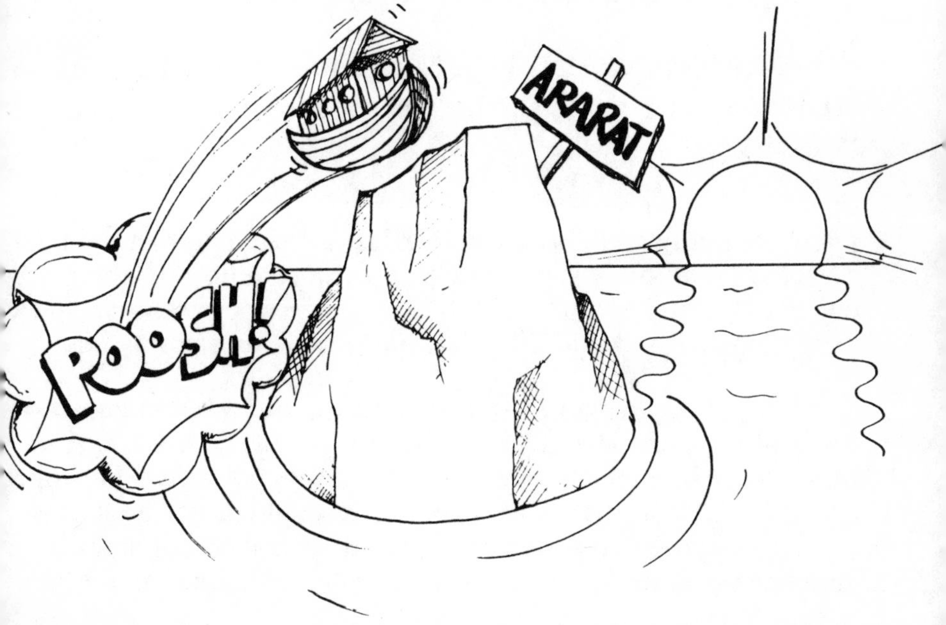
ARARAT
POOSH!

═══ WALLS OF JERICHO ═══

Many civilisations have been chastised by their neighbours on account of their rectal habits. The Children of Israel fall into this category.

Daddy Israel, very randy in his younger days, had bred a great many trumpeting children who formed a travelling band. However, at one of their gigs in Jericho, they were refused entry to the city until they tidied up their guffing act. Unhappy at the way they were being treated, The Children started sulking and fell silent.

Joshua, the lead singer, tried to cheer them up by taking them for walks around the city, until he got annoyed with the situation. In a fit of pique, he started shouting and farted into one of the band's horns. The Children thought this was a great laugh and started to copy him. To their amazement the walls of Jericho started to crumble, thus allowing the band in to do their first number.

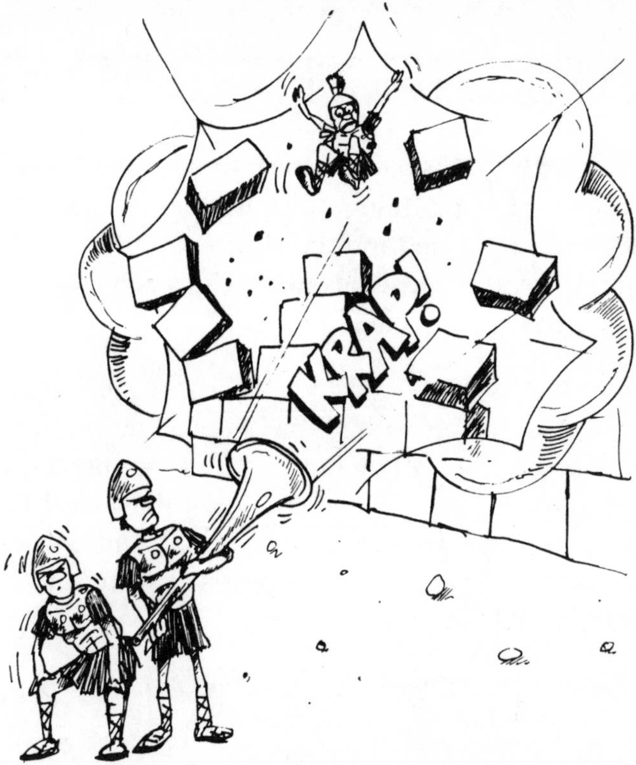
KRAP!

≡ PARPING THE RED SEA ≡

Moses and his mates had a pretty rough time when they went on holiday to Egypt. Being quite tolerant people they put up with the first 10 plagues and the slaying of all the first sons, but when gippy tummy* brought on by Egyptian food caused The Plague of Farts, they decided to leave.

Hotly pursued by the Egyptian Tourist Board (who thought Moses was running off with all the bog roll in the country), they found themselves cut off by the Red Sea. Unperturbed, Moses gathered all of his party into formation and asked for one last parping effort. Slowly the waves parted and Moses lead his party to safety. The pursuing Egyptians were all engulfed by the remaining tide of rear-end aroma.

* Sometimes called 'Pharaohs' Revenge', see also page 14.

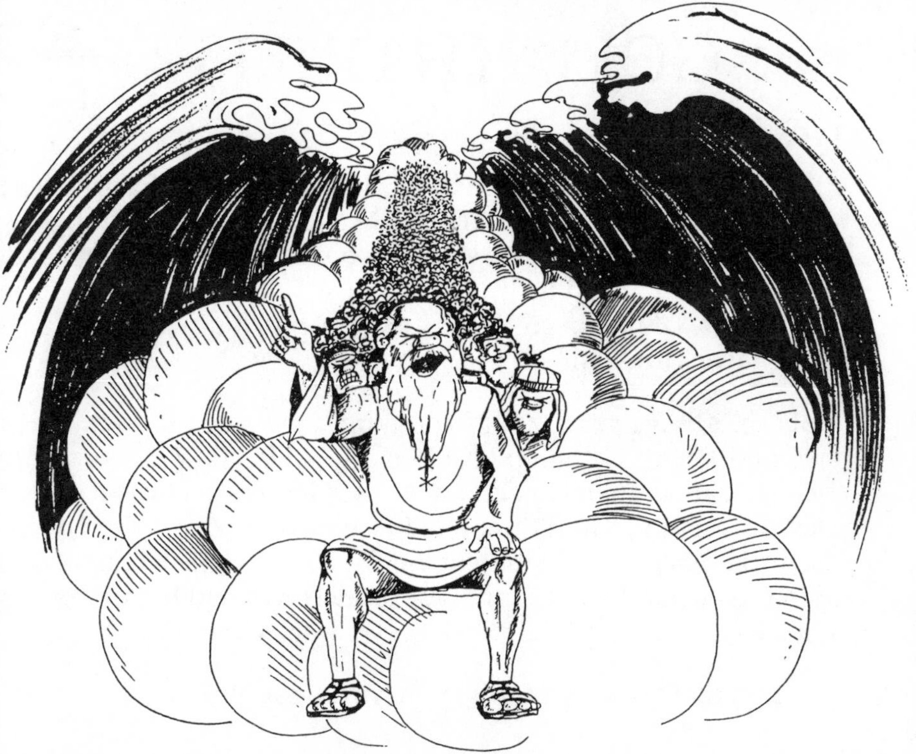

GOLIATH GUFFED

One of the earliest examples of the use of farts in open warfare is also depicted in 'The Bible According To St.Chuff'. The two armies involved are believed to have stopped fighting because of the suffering caused to innocent bystanders. Instead, they decided to send forward their best farters, to fart it out on the top of a hill where there was less possibility of innocents being farted to death.

Goliath, a huge man, could summon equally huge volumes of guff and stood as champion for many weeks until he came up against a small man called David. Not impressed by the size of David's rectum, Goliath commenced with a relatively innocuous little blarp. He instantly paid for this mistake when he was felled by a small hard round guff that David had been brewing since having a curry in Jerusalem two weeks before.

Big men don't always produce the strongest farts.

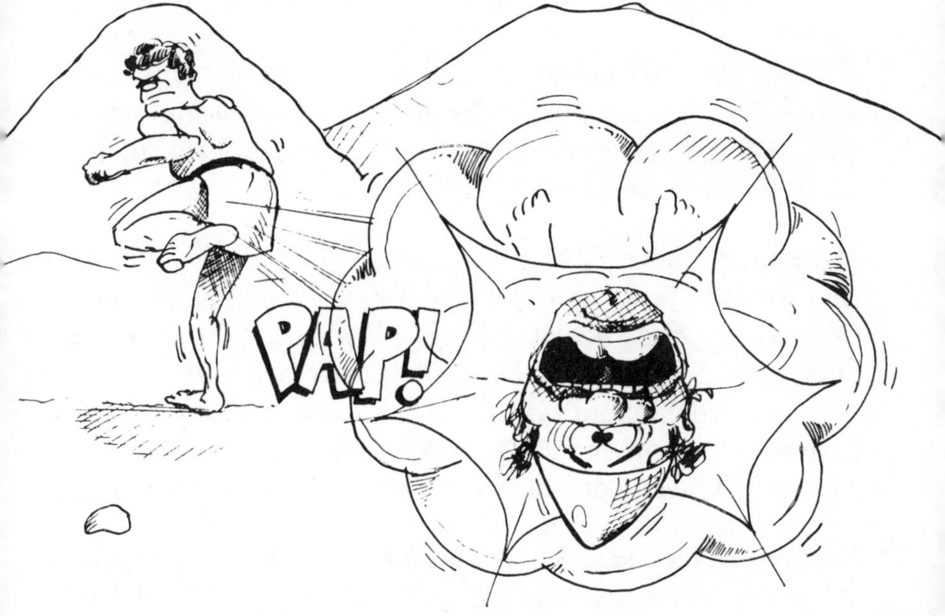
PAP!

═ GOR - GOD OF GUFFS ═

The Greeks are known to have worshipped many gods, of whom Zeus was believed to be the 'God of Gods' as well as the God of Wind. However, new evidence suggests that there may have been an even more powerful god.

Mythologists have discovered artifacts that could depict GOR, who was the brother of Thor and God of Guffs. A statue of GOR shows him with little wings for getting rid of the noxious fumes being emitted almost continuously from an impressively big arse. No ears are evident on the statue, although these may have been lost over time. It could also be that GOR didn't have ears so that he couldn't hear the complaints of his fellow gods.

Next time someone says to you at a party, "Gor, have you guffed?". It actually means that they are comparing you to a Greek God.

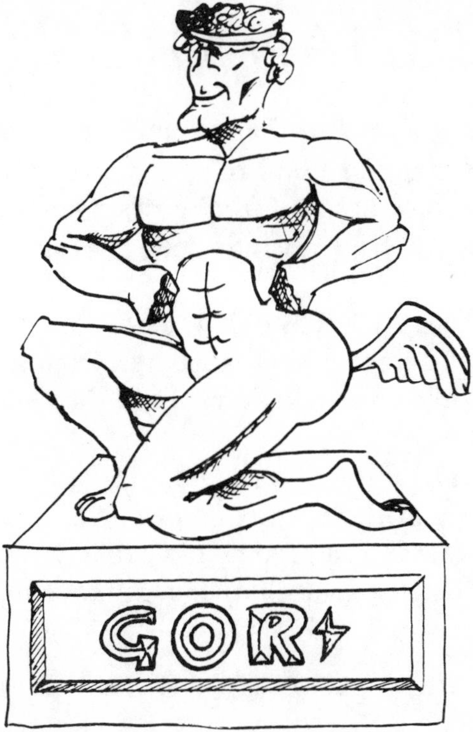
GOR

TROJAN TRUMP

Many of the myths told by the ancient Greeks are clouded in mystery, not to mention the Greek alphabet, and could hold vital clues to the ancient art of farting. Two new possible translations of the classics have recently been published:-

Jason and the Fartonauts tells of how Jason and his gallant band battled against skeletons (which appeared from a puff of guff) and a multi-bottomed beast, to bring home The Golden Fart.

Homer's Chuffiad, on the other hand, tells of the seige of Troy in which Helen (in mythology the first woman to fart) was being held captive. A horse captured by the Trojans let rip with such an obnoxious cha-doof that all of the city's inhabitants fled to save their lives.

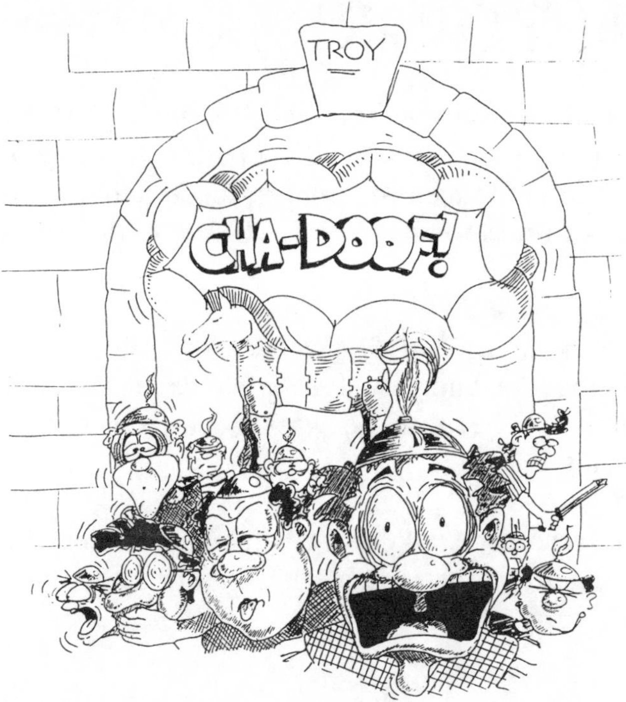
TROY
CHA-DOOF!

YOU-REEK-A

After a night out on the bevy with his mates, Archimedes, famous for his screws, was lying in the bath recovering from his hangover when he noticed the effervescence bubbling from his back-side. He promptly jumped out of the bath and ran into the street crying "Eureka ! Eureka !" or "I have it ! I have it !"

Whether Archimedes had discovered the true secret of the fart, or whether he had just discovered he had the clap, we shall never know because he was promptly run over by a passing chariot.

Present day scientists talk about The Archimedes Principle, which states that "A fart, when immersed in a crowd, will displace more than it's own volume of people."

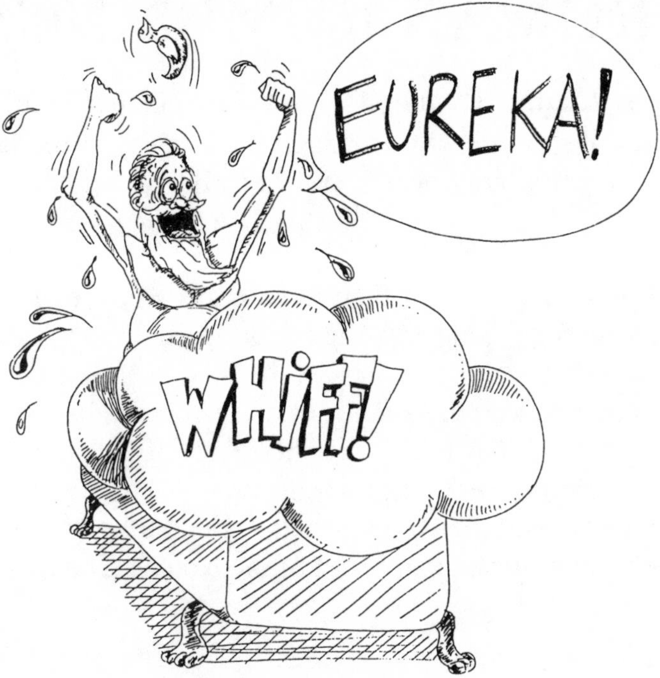
EUREKA!
WHIFF!

═ ROMAN RUMBLINGS ═

The rise of the Roman Empire can be attributed to the discovery of the secrets of farting hidden away at the back of a rather dimly lit pizza house in northern Italy.

Although the empire didn't last too long on an evolutionary scale, it was long enough for the Romans to develop a special type of nose for coping with their fetid farts.

Roman soldiers were known for wearing skirts in battle. It is still unclear what this has to do with the secret of farting but women wear skirts and they don't fart (do they ?). The Scots also wore skirts in battle and the Romans had to build a wall to keep them and their squarking bagparps out of the Roman Empire.

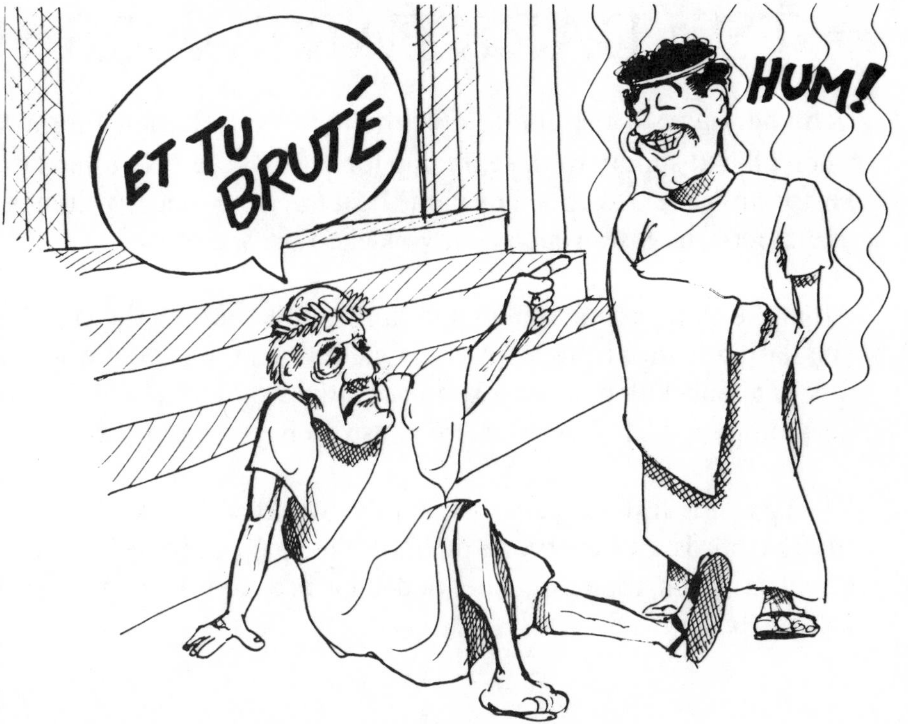
ET TU BRUTÉ
HUM!

= THE DARK FART AGES =

The dark ages came about after the fall of the Roman Empire when all and sundry went searching for the lost secrets of farting. Historians gave this epoch its name because of the sheer volumes of malodorous gases which nearly blocked out the sun.

Atilla the Pong was actually quite a nice fella but for the stench emanating from his underpants. One day he took them off for washing, and killed several representatives of The Hun Cleaning Company Ltd. Ever since, he has received a bad press.

Vikings set sail to tell everybody about their wonderful smörgåsbords, but everyone mistook the smell of their herrings for farts. Even today, red headed men are known to produce fishy farts.

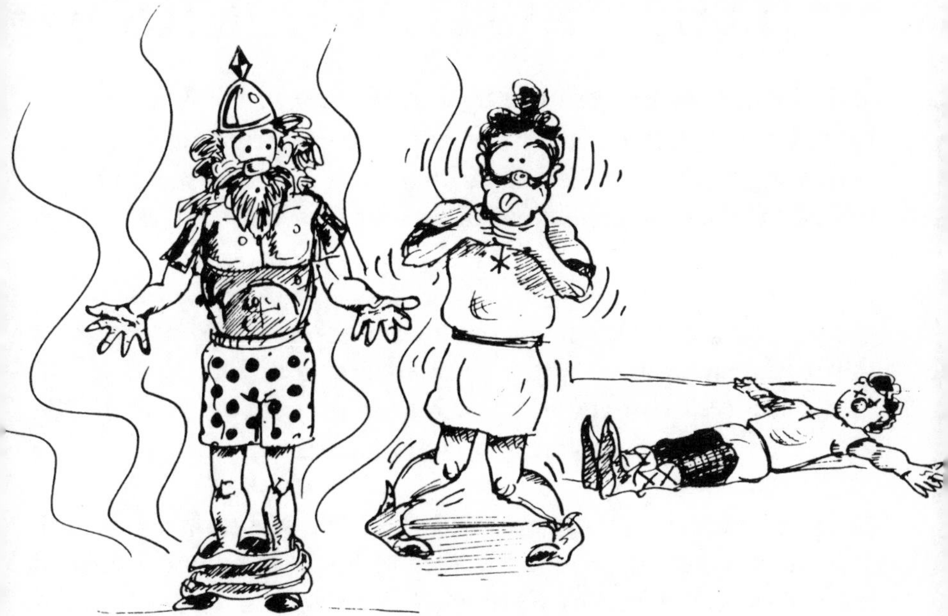

THE CROTCHADERS

Rumblings were heard throughout Europe in the Middle Ages which could be attributed to the invention of casked ale. It caused yet another bunch of die-hard trumpers to set off in search of the solution to their rectal distress. This time they were led by Richard The Lionfart under the banner of "Deus lo chuff".

More than one session on the razz had engineered the myth that the answer lay in either a chalice called 'The Holy Gruff' or in an old transport container called 'The fart of the Covenant' (later discovered by Indianus Jones).

Despite several package trips down to the Med, once with the kids, the Crotchaders failed to find either artifart and returned home to sign the Magna Farta at Runnypeed.

═ THE 100 YEARS FART ═

The Frogs, led by Philip Augustypants, on the other hand, reckoned the Brits had found the secret to farting whilst out on one of the crusades and promptly declared war.

So long and so hard was the farting during this war, they totally missed the fact that they actually continued farting for 116 years and not 100 years. One of the major victories by Britain was gained at Agincourt when they introduced the long blap to decimate the French after they caught them in the bog.

At the end of the war the Brits captured Joan of Fart who was reputedly a French resistance leader who could set fire to her own rippers. However, she did herself in when having her last smoke before going to the gallows (pronounced 'gauloise' in French).

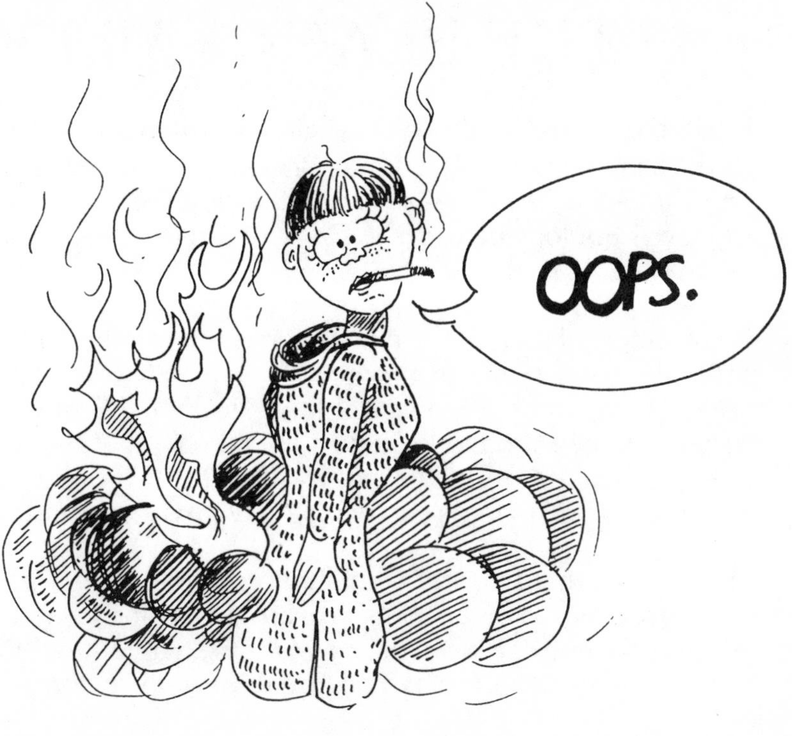
OOPS.

THE BLACK FART

Historians believe The Black Fart (medically known as Killus Gufforium) was introduced into Britain by a rat flea-ing from a ship's tom-cat. The tom-cat had not seen a she-cat for six years and it was not long before The Black Fart had spread throughout the land.

Those infected found their farts turning more and more fetid until one day they would produce a completely black fart which would be so strong it would kill them instantly. Gangs of bum-doctors roamed around calling on everybody to "bring out your farts". When they found anybody with a slightly greying fart they would lock them indoors and paint a red cross on the entrance.

Around this time, a fatal combination of black farts produced in a baker's shop in London proved too explosive and caught fire. Guff fumes all over the capital were ignited and the incident has become known as The Great Fart of London.

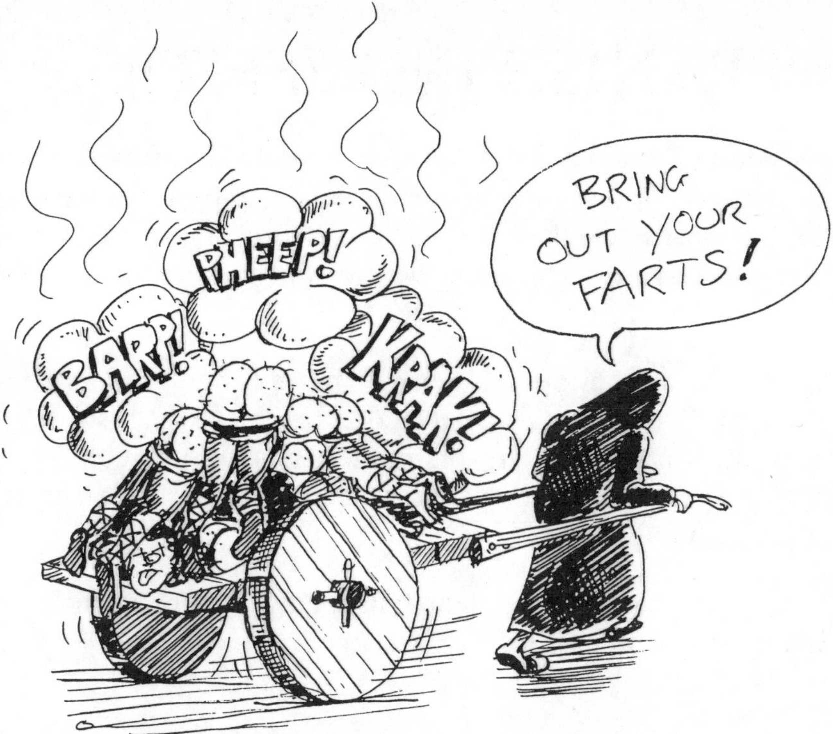

PHEEP!
BARP!
KRAK!
BRING OUT YOUR FARTS!

≡ SPANISH INGUFFITION ≡

Absolutely nobody expected The Spanish Inguffition. Sent out by the Parpacy, and under the leadership of Torquefarta, the Spaniards searched for and tortured all those who would confess to farting. This purge was originally started in an effort to secure the secrets of farting for the Vatican.

Many sinister contraptions were employed to get their victims to admit to farting. These included the rack which stretched farts out of people, the pinion which steered people into farting and the red hot poker which was used to detect any lingering fumes.

Next time you drop a 'silent but deadly' watch out for The Spanish Inguffition.

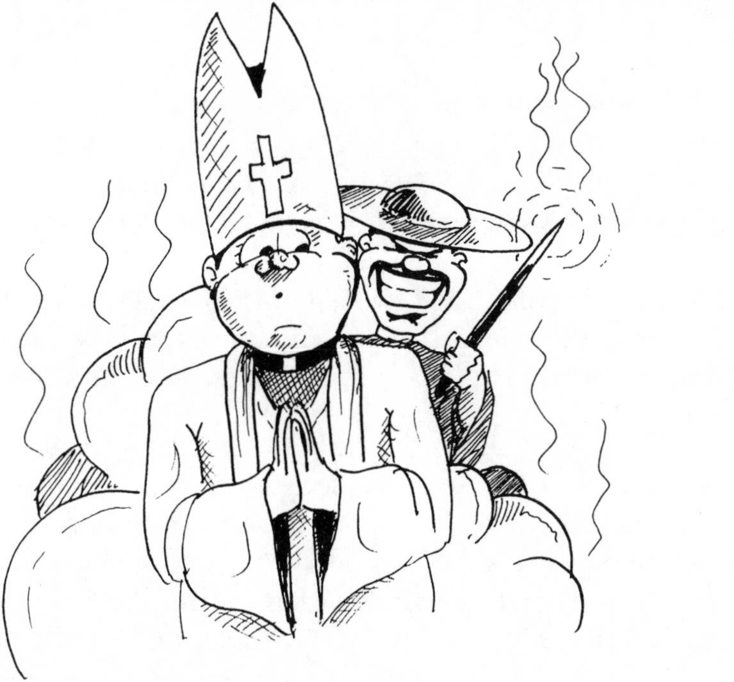

= CHINESE FIREWORKS =

While everybody in Europe was actively searching for the secret powers of farting, the Chinese believed that farts carried evil spirits. Most Chinese would try to hold their farts in, so they would not be thought of as being evil. As a result, when a small fart escaped it sounded more like a whisper than a thunderclap. Anyone caught whispering in public would be talked about by their friends. These days the process of talking about other people's farts is known as Chinese Whispers.

In order to cut down on the total amount of evil guff in the country, the Chinese have decreed that no-one should have more than one fart. If anyone feels an unofficial fart coming on then they are ordered to go down to the people's firework factory and make a contribution to the cultural revolution. Confucius he say ... evil brews in another man's underpants.

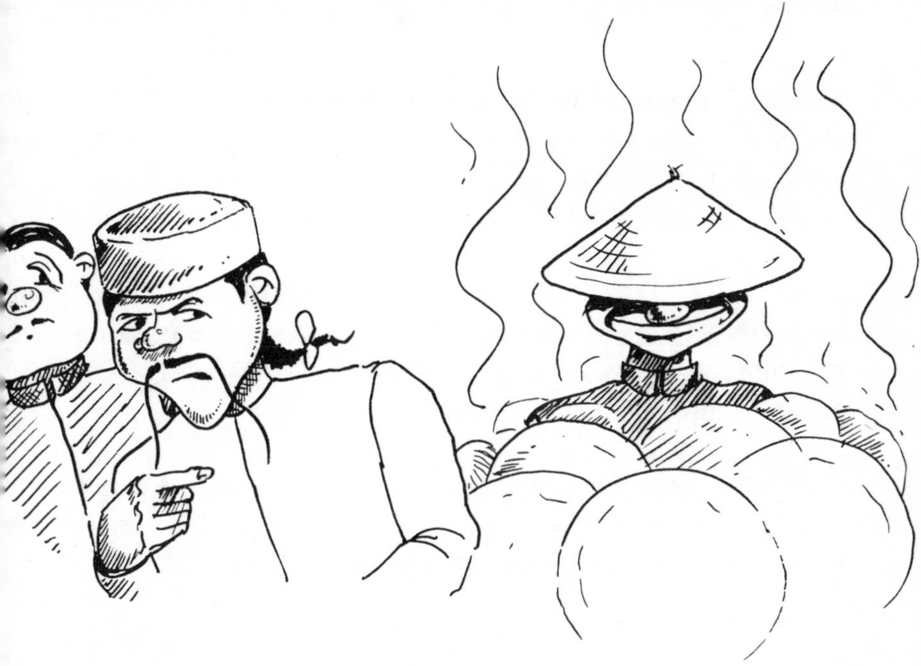

SILLY CNUT

King Cnut II reckoned that everything on the planet was within his power and, with his friend Edmund Ironfarts, he could control everything by his parping prowess.

After a few too many lagers in the sun, this unlikely pair found themselves on the beach and Cnut took up a bet from Ironfarts. Trousers dropped, he took aim at the ocean and as the tide came in he tried to make it retreat with a series of bottom blaps.

Of course the sea didn't stop and Cnut ended up with the cleanest arse in the land. The rest of his reign was marked by the bubbling noises of his newly patented frothy farts.

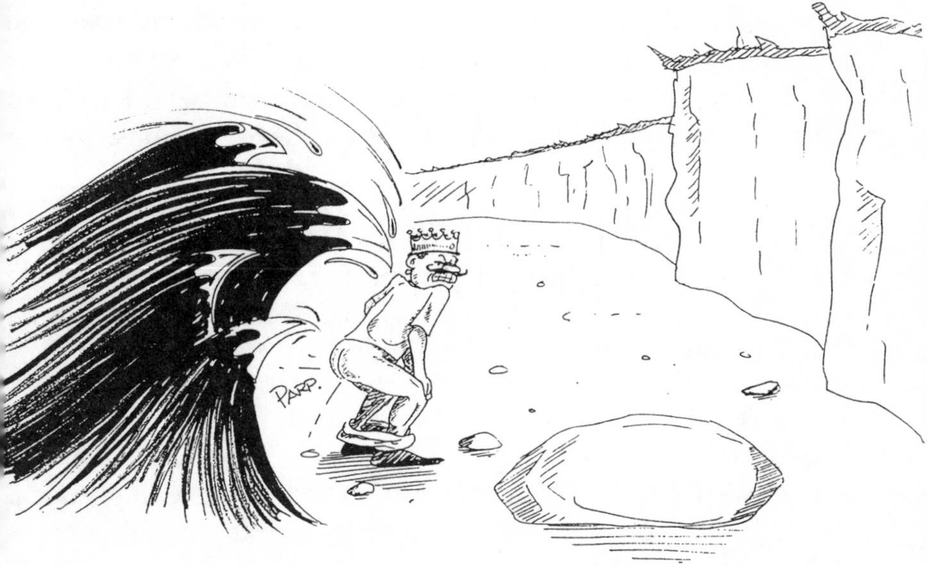
PARP.

TURIN SHROUDER

Many scientists and historians have tried to find out when and how the Turin Shroud came to be. We can now disclose, thanks to new technology, that the Shroud may have been imprinted when a battle-weary knight called Ed was towelling himself down after having a nice warm shower with his fellow knights.

Unfortunately, Ed was stood behind a particularly flatulant knight and got caught by a real blaster. The only thing that saved Ed was his towel which was forced against him so hard that it became imprinted with his features.

The technology which made this explanation possible is called Radioactive Farton Dating. Each fart is slighly radioactive and decays with a half-life inversly proportional to the importance of the person you are talking to at the time (ie: the more important the person, the longer the fart will stay).

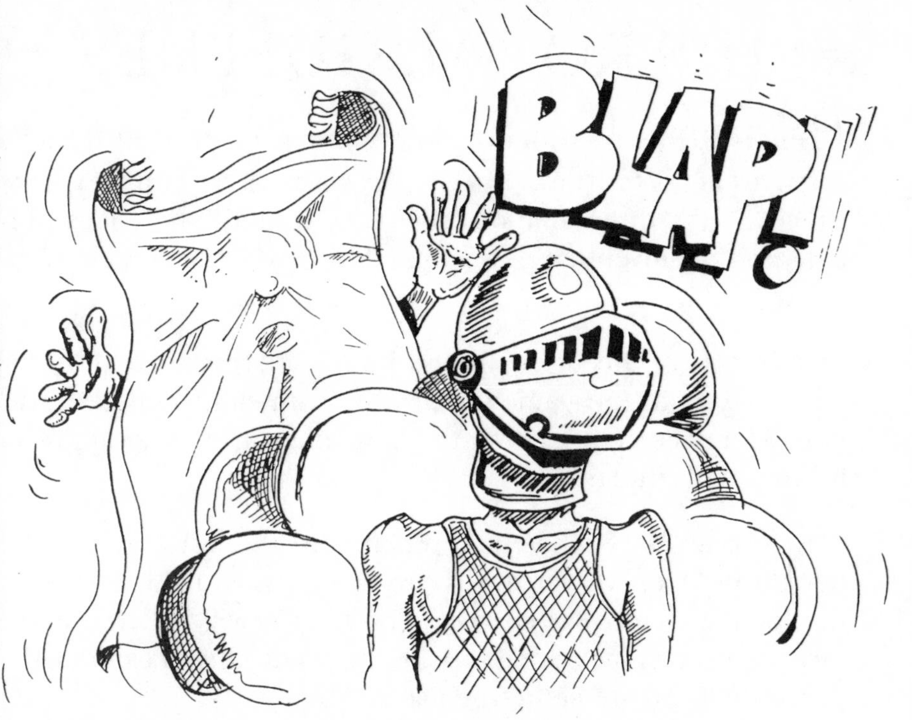
BLAP!

HIS ROYAL GUFFNES

Henry VIII was a rotund fellow and managed to get through six wives in his fart-time. Two of his wives died when they were caught in the direct line of his equally rotund farts. This precipitated the invention of the 'Cod Piece' which was used to redirect the fart and dissipate some of its power.

Two more of his wives were beheaded because of their infartelity and one gained a divorce with third degree burns after Henry came back with the boys and started setting fire to his rear-end rippers.

Any peasant slave who could remain fart-free for a year and a day during Henry's reign was given his own freedom. This is one of the main reasons why The Crown will still not allow farts, or even value-added farts, to be taxed. If you can't fart in peace then you are not a free man.

MOANING LISA

Leonardo da Vinci is well known as a great scientist and painter, but not many people know he suffered from Terminal Toots. The odour from toots created whilst he was painting still remain impregnated in The Moaner Lisa and that is why it has to be hung in The Loo-vre.

The model for The Moaner Lisa was obviously suffering, judging by the strained smile on her face. Some researchers suggest that Moaner's facial distortion may have been a result of holding one of her own farts in, but this can not be reconciled with the long standing theory that women don't fart.

Leo was also one of the first people to understand Inertia (the way in which farts hang around without moving) and this helped him invent the very first helicopter-fart. When used properly, these blasts can cause a person to levitate off the ground and hover in mid-guff for several minutes.

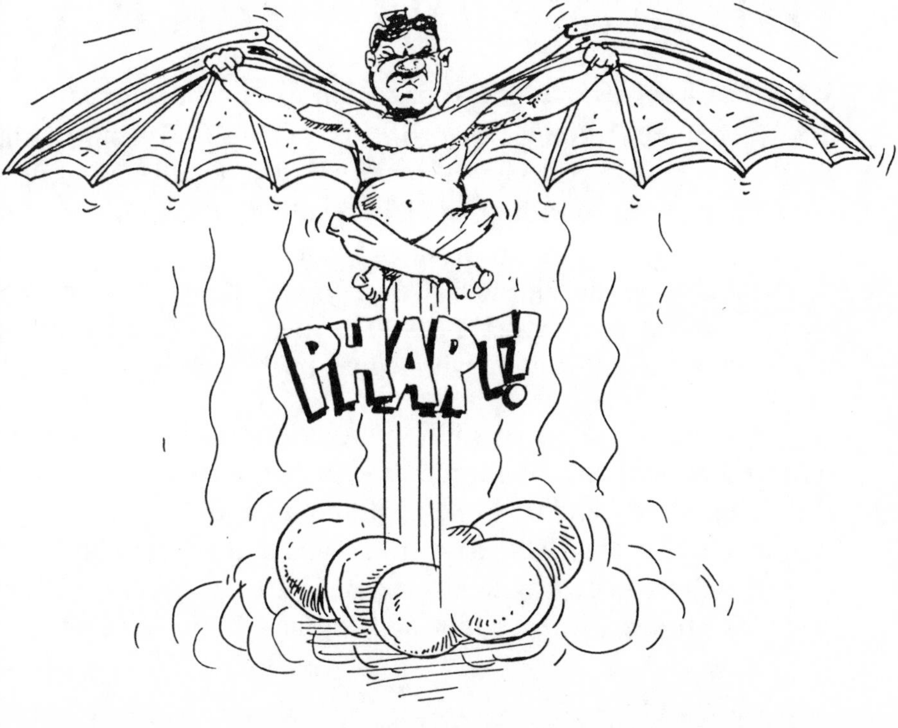
PHART!

THE BUM CHOWDER PLOT

Guy Fawkes was one of the first men to discover the extreme difficulty of performing the 'controlled chuff'. Living in the sticks, he was forced to eat a meagre diet of cabbage and eggs with prunes for pudding, which resulted in explosive side effects. Sick of this continual trouser ventilation, Fawkes embarked on an heroic suicide mission - to destroy Parliament with one of his own ignited farts. Stuffing himself on his staple diet, he set out for London with a cork pushed up his backside.

All went well. He successfully secreted himself in the cellars, removed his cork and lit a torch. But as the tension mounted his cheeks tightened, and try as he might nothing would pass his lips. A couple of passing Beefcurryeaters walked in to catch him bent double with his kegs around his ankles. These days we commemorate Guy's bravery with a controlled 'letting-off' of fireworks.

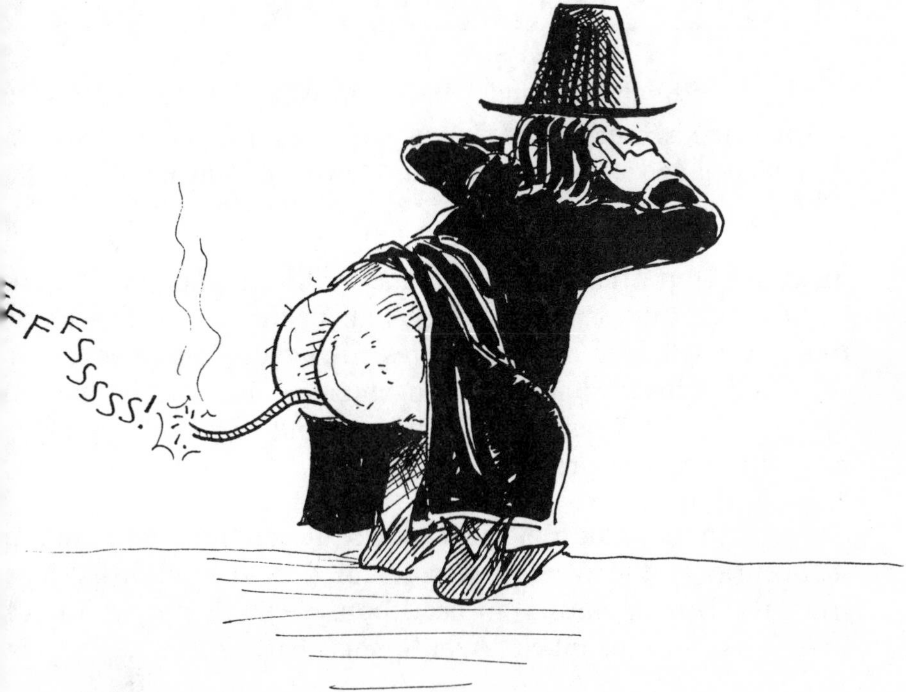
FFSSSSS!

≡ THE SPANISH ARMADA ≡

Philip II of Spain was under the impression that the Brits were keeping the secret art of farting under wraps. So he sent an Armada, loaded with galleons of fart power, to claim it for himself.

Drake first heard about this whilst he was outside playing with his balls. Unperturbed, he continued with the comment, "there is plenty of time to have a fart, and to thrash the Spaniards too". Raleigh, who had taken up smoking a pipe as a cover for the smell of his own anal announcements (caused by eating too many potatoes), would have helped out but Lizzy I chopped his head off for over trumping.

Trapped in the mouth of the Thames (a great effluent outlet in its own right), the Armada was defeated by several broadsides from the British ships who used bum-blasts to propel lots of little bowls into the much larger Spanish backsides.

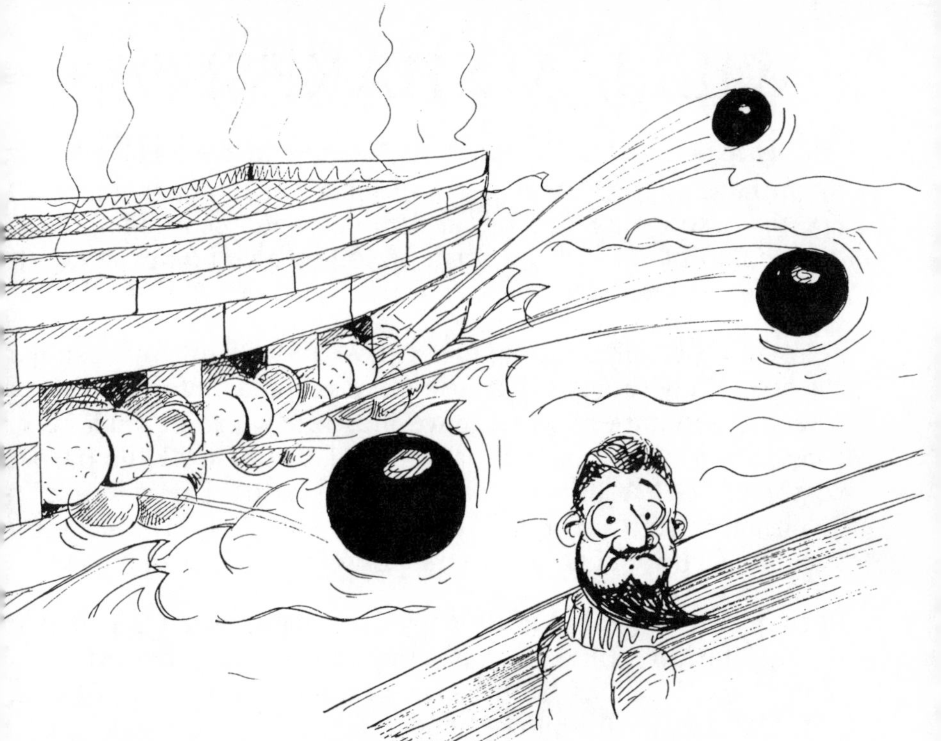

= WILLIAM SHAKESPOKE =

Willy, who lived in Stratfart-on-Avon with Anne Haveitaway might have been trying to trace the secret art of farting himself. He reworked many historical writings and recorded them in 'prone and blank farts', a form of code which he developed to cover up his research.

A review of 'The Complete Parps of William Shakespoke' suggests Willy thought that losing the secret art of farting was a tragedy. Quotations which have illustrated this for students of English through the years include; "Alas poor Jorik, he parped very well" - "A horse, a horse, you farted like a horse" - "Neither a guffer nor a chuffer be" and, fully aware of the travelling nature of acrid odours, "Beware the farts that march".

Perhaps the biggest clue to Willy's farting knowledge comes in the quotation "Blow, winds, and crack your cheeks! rage! blow!" which comes from 'Love's Labour's Lost' (III.ii.1) and not 'Much Apoo About Nothing'.

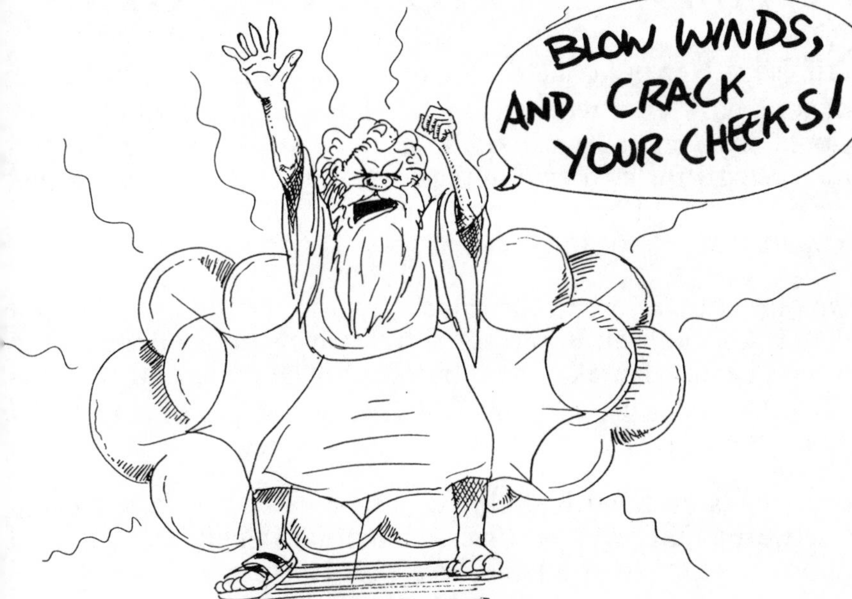
BLOW WINDS, AND CRACK YOUR CHEEKS!

≡ GRAVITATIONAL GUFFS ≡

Sir Isaac Newpong liked nothing better than a pint or fifteen of good dark stout with his lunch. The initial effect of the drink would be to make Isaac a bit dozy, so he would wander out into the orchard for a snooze in the sun. Later on, the brew would make its after effects felt, and Isaac would start trumpeting like a bandsman.

On one of these occasions Isaac's arsehole created such a blast that it knocked an apple off a tree which promptly fell onto Isaac's head. "Eureka" he shouted, until he realised that somebody else had already done that one (see page 28), so instead he invented gravity.

Once his sore head had cleared, Isaac got down to work and discovered that every positive action of farting has an equal and opposite reaction from the inhaler. This is more simply described by the equation $F = M \times A$ where F is the Fart Force, M is the Mass of Beer drunk and A is the Acridity Coefficient.

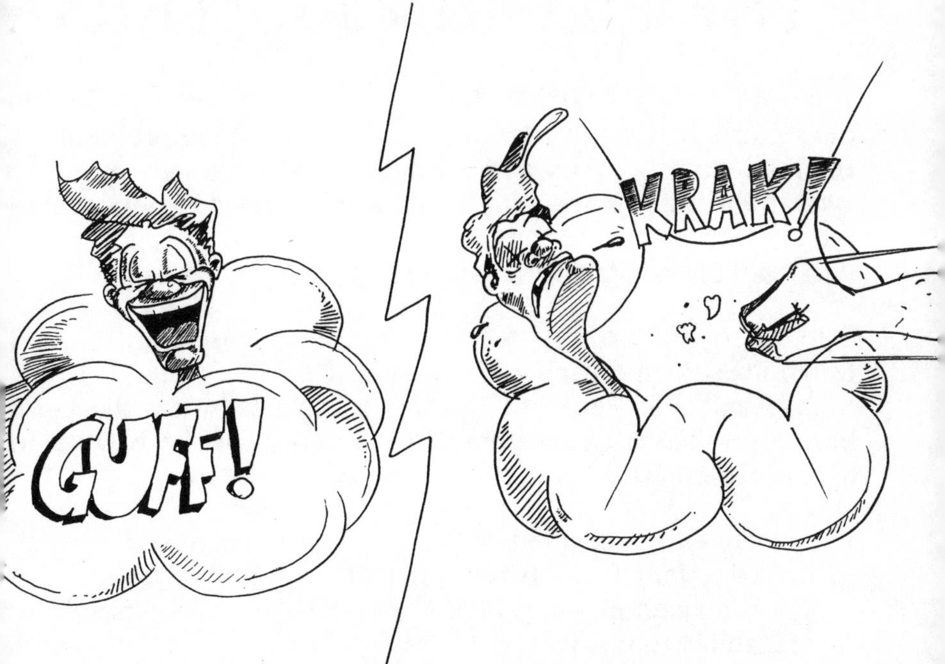
GUFF!
KRAK!

≡ THE PILGRIM FARTERS ≡

Plymouth, being at the bottom of the country, is where all the dense farts sink down to; thus causing a bad smog problem for the inhabitants. To try and rid the town of toxic trumps at the start of the 17th Century, the authorities decided to deport everybody with rancid rectums before they could have children and pass on their gas-generating genes.

The deported fathers set sail in the sarcastically named Mayflower to find a new life in America. Unfortunately they found that they were not the first people to settle the land, because someone had beaten them to it by flying the Atlantic in a giant balloon filled with hot hummers.

Undeterred they decided to farm a new breed of fowl which produced a pong from its rear end with a 'gobbling' noise. The turkey is now eaten every year by Americans as a thanksgiving for the ability to fart in a free land.

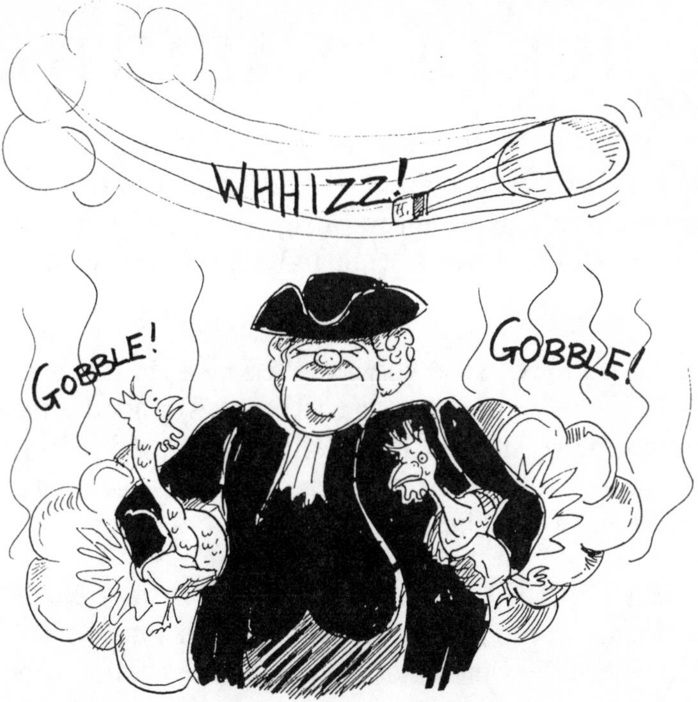
WHHIZZ!
GOBBLE!
GOBBLE!

BATTLE OF TRAFARTGER

Lord Hofartio Nelson was chosen to repel the combined farting forces of France and Spain at Cape Trafartger. At the start of the battle, Nelson sent a signal in semiparp by igniting his copious chuffs; it read "England expects every bowel to do its duty".

A little later in the battle he was felled by a short sharp squeak from a Frenchie in the crows nest. Lying wounded on the floor he said to his right hand man "Kiss me Hardy". Hardy's response to this request was a well known phrase or saying, which can not be re-printed here.

Rumour has it that Nelson continued to fart after his death, so he was incarcerated in concrete and put on top of a column in London where the wind could take away the volatile vapours.

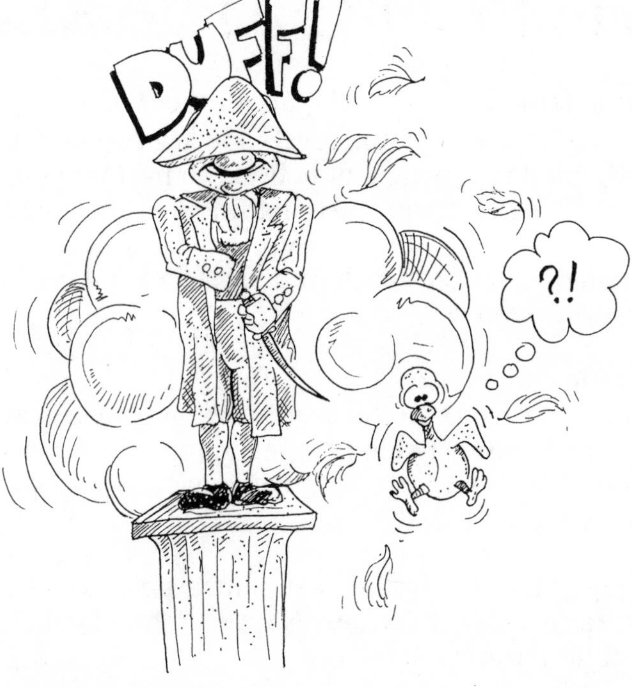
DUFF!
?!

= BATTLE OF FARTERLOO =

It is a little known fact that Naparpleon Bonafart was plagued with excessive gaseous emissions. He overcame this embarrassing situation by having a pipe fitted to his rear end. Passing between his legs, it was terminated in a stop-cock which enabled him to contain his flatulence until a convenient moment when he would reach into his jacket and gently release the noxious substance.

However, he came unstuck at the Battle of Farterloo when up against his arch rival the Puke of Wellington. A stray cannon shell exploded closely behind Nappy and blew away his plumbing. The subsequent stench overpowered the poor little Frenchies and all was lost.

Now unregulated, his farting was unbearable, and the British were forced to exile the luckless Nappy to the island of Elba for the rest of his natural emissions.

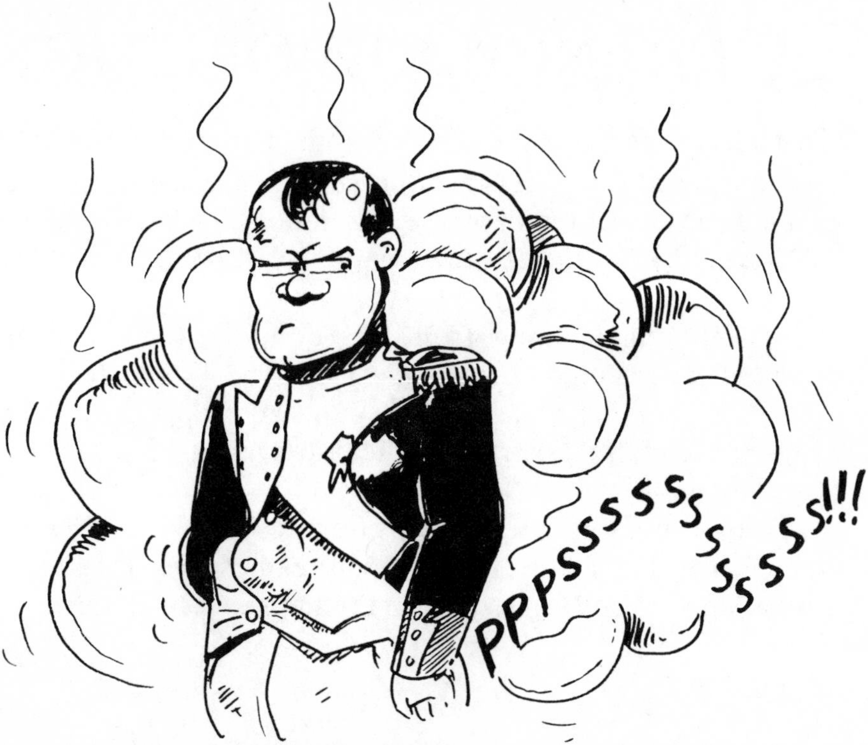
PPPSSSSSSSSSSSSSS!!!

LE FRENCH REVOLUTION

Just why les peasants were so revolting is, of course, hidden in le underpants of les French. But when le parping plebs complained to Royalty that it was le rotten diet which was creating le stink on le streets, they were completely ignored.

Upon inhaling le pong from her boudoir, Marie Av-ye-trumped-yet declared "Let them eat Curry". This really got le goat of les working classes and they started chopping off a few têtes with le motto 'Liberte! Egalite! Farternite'.

Only one person could help Les Royals - Le Scarlet Pumpernel! He had been a lifelong friend of Dick Turpin and always stood to deliver, usually on the steps to le guillotine.

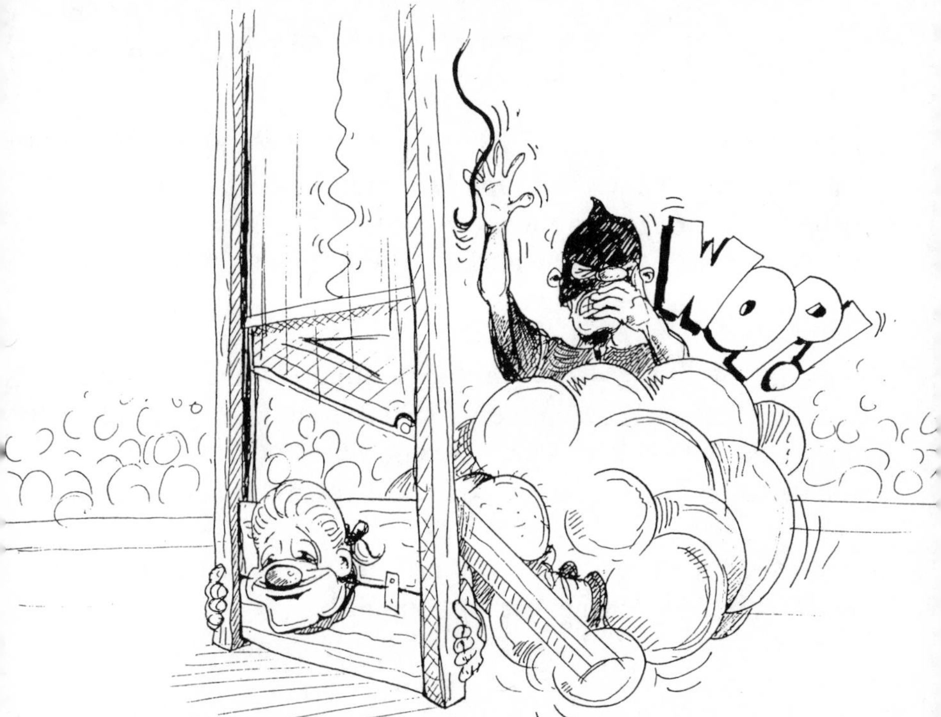
WOP!

BELLE EPOQUE

Les Frogs really got going during le Belle Epoque when they reckoned that they had found le secret art de farting. Le philosopher Desfartes announced "I fart, therefore I'm man" to which le whole country replied "he-hore, he-hore, he-hore" without moving their cheeks.

Dans le countryside they put les farts into le cheap plonk and created Champagne, une very expensive plonk. Whilst dans le city de Paris they built une tower designed by Eiffel for tous le monde to go up and guff in front of all les American tourists.

Had they found le secret ? Mais non, it was just a side effect from eating too much garlic and onions !

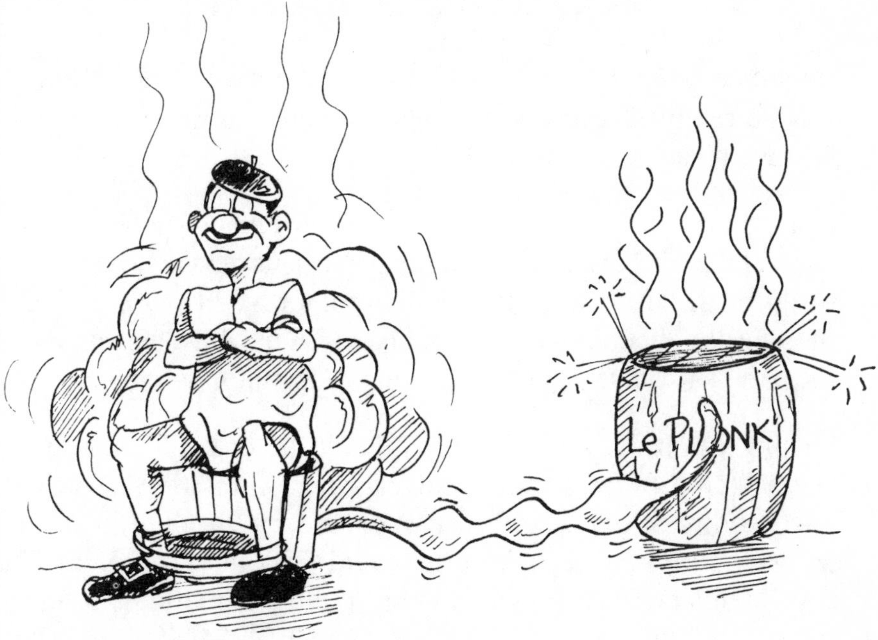
Le PL NK

ROYAL FLUSH

Thomas Crapper was not a big hit with the ladies. Not only was he really Thomas in bed, but a cloud of fetid fumes always followed his every movement.

In an attempt to increase his chances, he invented a machine which would hide his flatulence from the girls. This device he called the flush toilet. However, his luck didn't improve because he found that absolutely no females would talk to him whilst he was sat on the pan. The only thing that he managed to pull was a chain.

His invention did a bit better in the world of commerce and it was selected as the winning entry in the Tommorow's World of Farts competition. The Prince of Gales was the chief judge and he decided that everyone in the country should have one. This royal connection explains why the toilet is sometimes referred to as 'The Throne'.

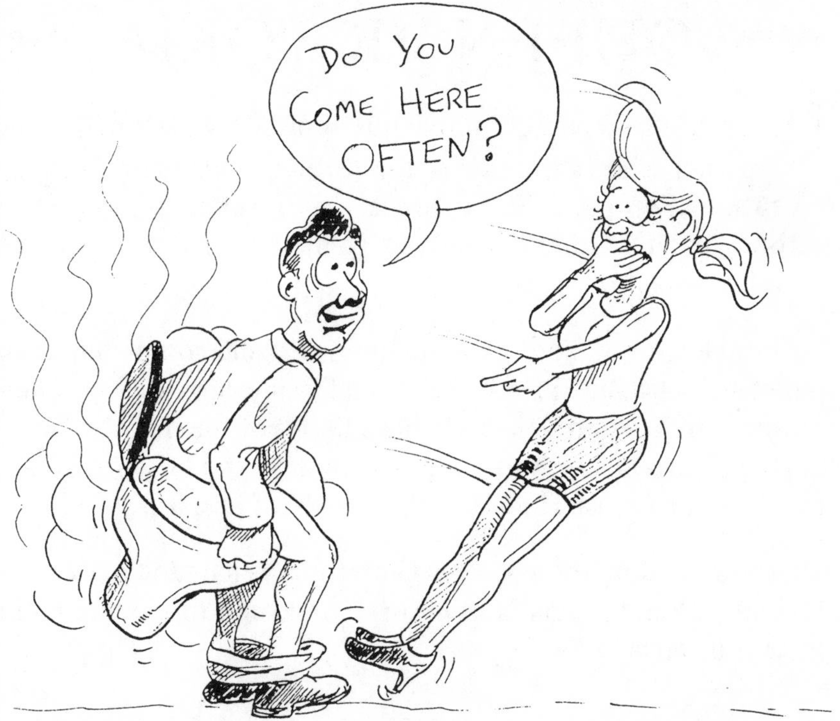
DO YOU COME HERE OFTEN?

QUEEN VICTORIA

Queen Victoria was definitely not amused by the smells which greeted her when she came to the throne. Following Crapper's invention (See page 70), a succession of males had sat on the throne, each of them majestically murmuring away in their scuddies whilst ruling the land.

As a revenge for these male mannerisms, she completely dominated her husband Prince Alfart and made him go and build a museum in London. She also chased a lot of the more volumous male guff producers away from the country, and they were forced to set up the British Empire with the help of Disfarti.

Victoria is said to have put her long reign down to never farting. Wouldn't you be a miserable old sod too, if you had to hold your farts in for 64 years ?

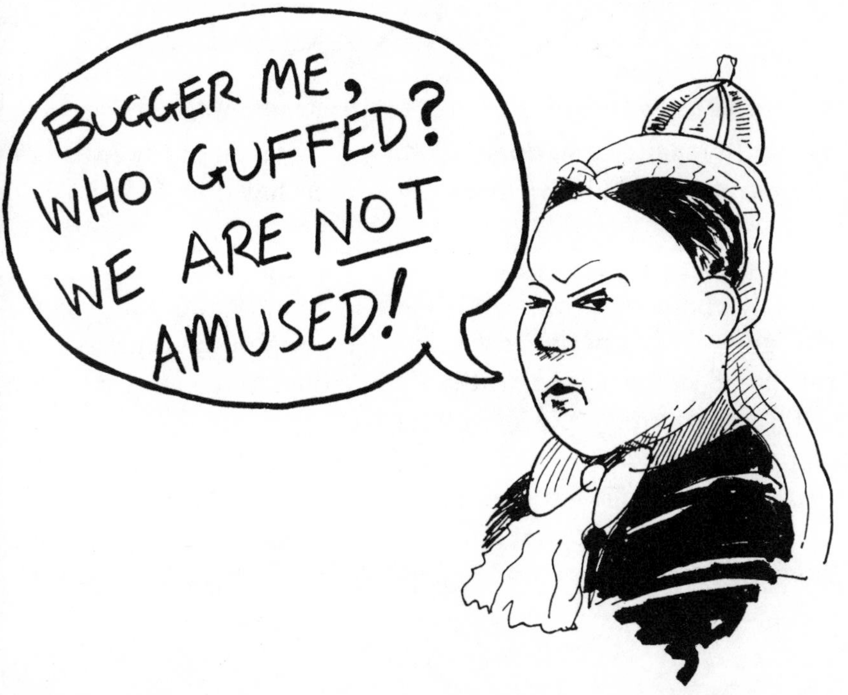
BUGGER ME, WHO GUFFED? WE ARE NOT AMUSED!

THE SUFARTGETTES

From 1918 every adult in the country who could fart was given a vote in local and national elections. This naturally precluded women who had always maintained that they didn't fart.

In an effort to force the vote upon women, some females were forcibly chained to rails and buildings until it was thought they had guffed. In another case, one lady was pushed in front of a racehorse in the hope that the fright would make her fart. None of these measures were successful.

Women eventually got their vote when it was discovered that the amount of flatulence seeping from a female's pores in any one day is approximately equal in mass to a really big cushion duster.

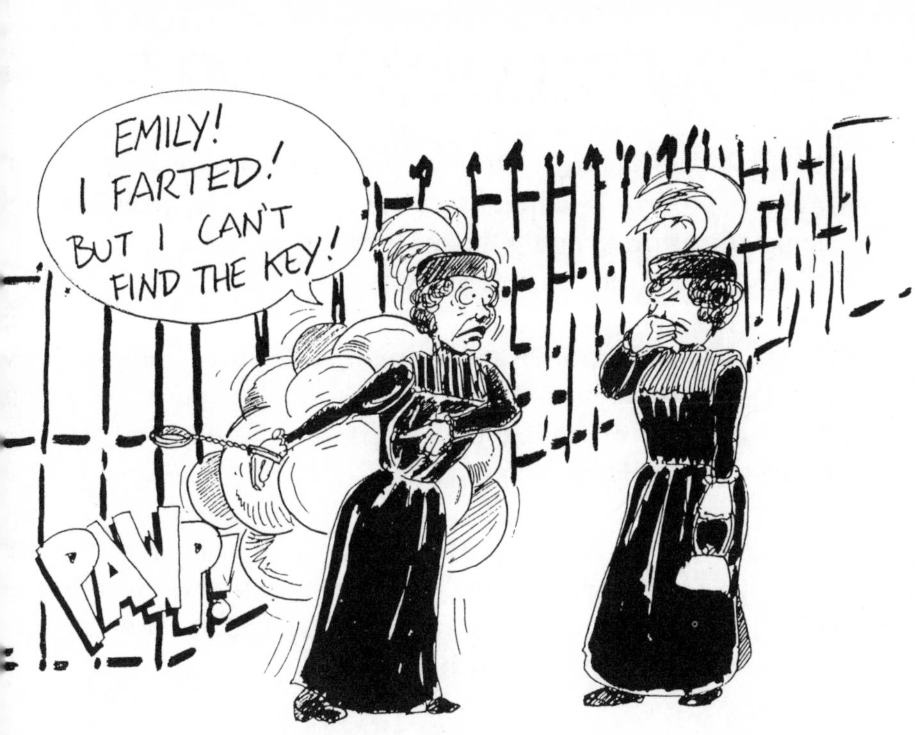
EMILY! I FARTED! BUT I CAN'T FIND THE KEY!
PAWP!

SHERLOCK FUMES

Sherlock was a real character, based on fiction, who went around detecting if people had farted or not. He specialised in tracing and apprehending the parpitrators of killer farts, poison farts and farts with a twist in the tail.

One of the most complicated cases that he managed to solve was 'The Hummer of the Baskervilles'. In this story he is commonly quoted to have uttered those immortal words, "Alimentary my Dear Whatfart".

Sherlock finally met his demise when he tried to arrest Professor Moreafarty on the edge of a cliff. He dropped a guffer himself and the reaction (see page 58) propelled him over the edge and into a waterfall.

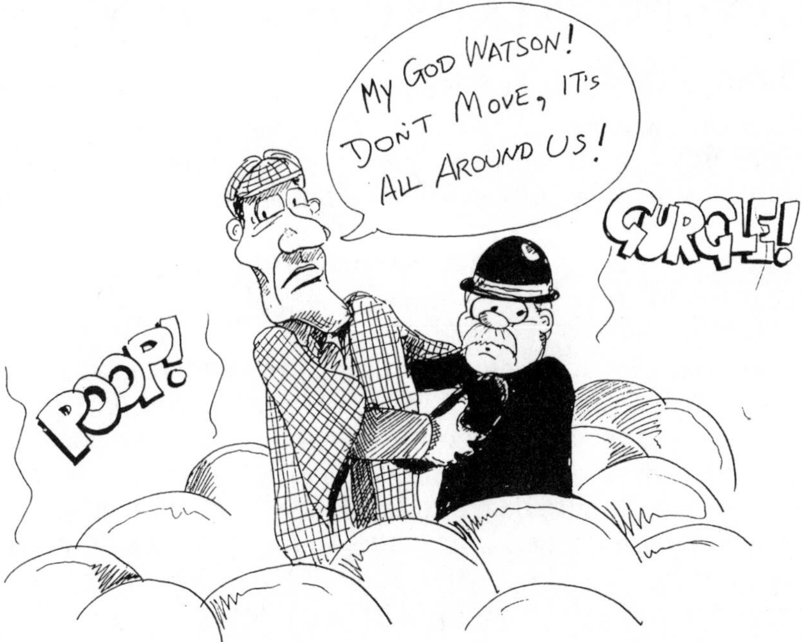
MY GOD WATSON! DON'T MOVE, IT'S ALL AROUND US!
POOP!
GURGLE!

LIVINGSTONE & STANLEY

Doctor Livingstone had gone to Africa to do research for his thesis on the chuffing habits of chimpanzees. When he was there, he was captured by the tribe of Canyballs (horrible people who sniff their own farts), but luckily his rectal steak was so disgusting that they refused to eat him. In fact, so overpowering was the pong, that the tribe made him their leader, or Great Fharta as he became known.

Various parties were sent to look for Livingstone, one of them was headed by 'Stanley the Sniffer'. On one of Sniffer's probes deep into the jungle, he too was caught by the Cannyballs. In order to save his own life, Stanley had to prove that he knew Livingstone. Blindfolded, Stanley was lead into the village with the whole tribe gathered around. Then, with complete accuracy, Stanley walked straight up to the Great Fharta and shook him by the underpants saying "Dr Livingstone, I presume !"

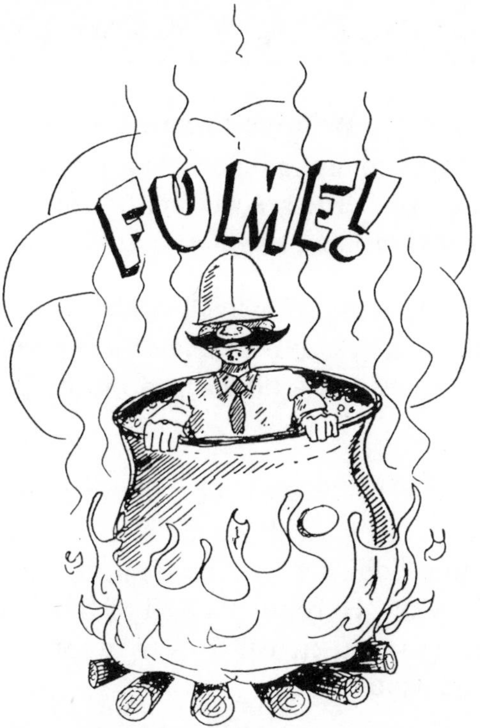
FUME!

═ CUSTER'S LAST FART ═

Anything went in the Wild West where the carrying of hand fart and rifled farts was common place. This farting freedom lead to many shoot outs in order to see who was the quickest farter on the draw, or who could produce the most accurate parp over distance

The influx of Carpet Baggers, selling fart water to the indians caused the authorities to push the various tribes onto reserves Naturally the indians got a bit wazzed off at this and created a real stink.

Custer was sent in to quieten them down a bit. However, he was sniffed out, along with all his men, at the battle of Little Big Horny when the indians encircled them in a ring of guff produced with a cry of "Geronimo". All of those who stood their ground where covered in carry-over, apart from one horse which remained white.

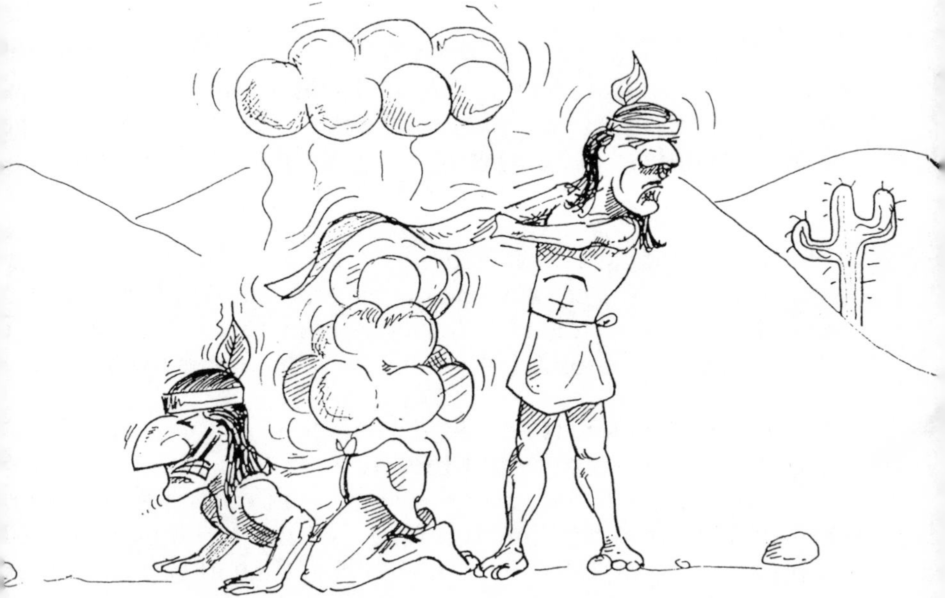

THE TELE-FART

Edison and Bell realised there was a need to communicate their farts over distances which made mere diffusion too slow. They found themselves cheek-to-cheek in the race to be first to develop a tele-farting system with Ralph & Huey who re-designed the toilet into a 'Great White Telephone'.

The first noise heard down every telephone around the world for many years was the crackling rasp of a pre-recorded fart. Similar to a fax machine, the fart-tone was used to establish contact between the two 'phones before anybody could talk down them.

Technology has now rendered the fart-tone obsolete on everything but the walkie-talkie. Modern communications make use of optical farters to increase the number of odours that can be carried down any one line at a time. Before too long it should be possible to smell the person who is guffing at you as well as hearing them.

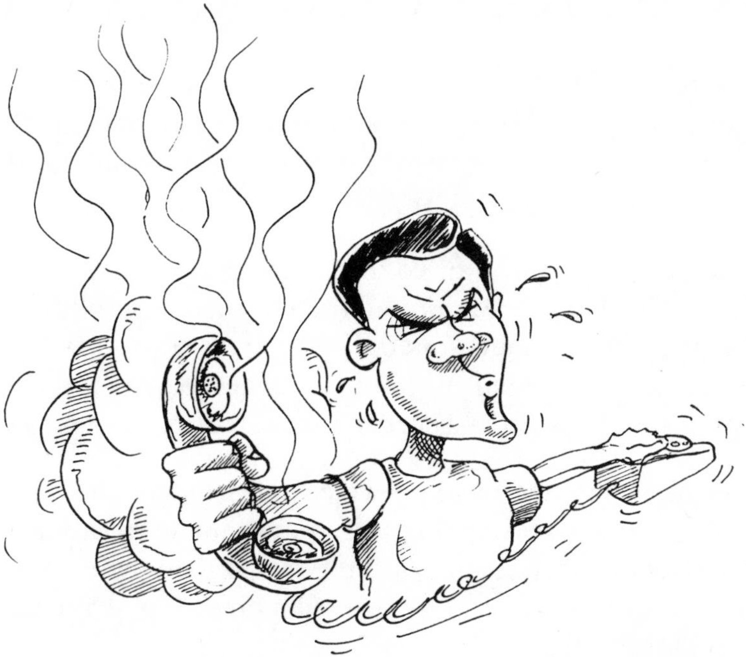

BERMUDA TRUMPANGLE

Silent But Deadly (SBD) is the term applied to a fart which wears carpet slippers and creeps up on its victims totally unannounced. In some areas of the world these sour shufflers are an endemic species.

One of these areas is contained within a triangle close to Bermuda where large ships and whole squadrons of planes have disappeared without a trace. Although some people report seeing a vague cloud of guff, it is believed that the pilots and captains were taken unawares by great swarms of gagged guffs.

The most famous incident which occurred in this area came when a short ship's chef served supper made from local beans. An SBD eased itself out of the pot and the whole crew had to abandon ship before they were overcome. This ship was called The Marie Celeste.

SCOTT OF THE ANFARTIC

Scott and four companions were involved in a race with Aguffson to become the first people to freeze dry a fart at the South Pole. The final product was to be used to give packet coffee a distinctive aroma when first opened.

Aguffson is believed, by some, to have won the race by using huskies to humm across the ice, instead of horses who are expensive at the pumps.

One of Scott's companions, who was well known for his elongated endurance parps, got lost one night when he went out for a quick puff. He had only told the team that he "may be some time".

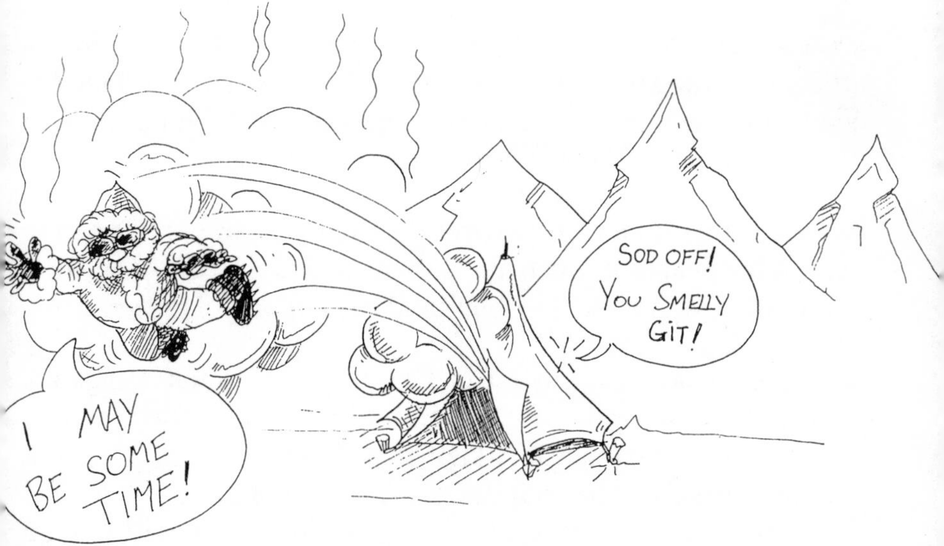
SOD OFF! YOU SMELLY GIT!
I MAY BE SOME TIME!

═ WALL STREET CHUFF ═

No-one realised the full implications when Ivan dropped a little squeaker on the trading floor in Wall Street. In fact no-body paid any interest at all until they realised the inflation rate of the Trump was larger than expected.

As this rectal rumour spread over the exchange, traders started to make a big deal of it which made them all feel a bit SEAQ. Their only option was to bid "buy-buy" and to jump out of the window.

A similar incident occurred in October 1987 when a gigantic great guff caused gales in the South of England. The resulting fart-exchange crash became known as 'Black Monday' after the opaque nature of the anal gases. Although no-one has admitted responsibility for this faux pas, it is widely accepted to be a result of 'The Big Bang' when traders set fire to their own farts on the floor.

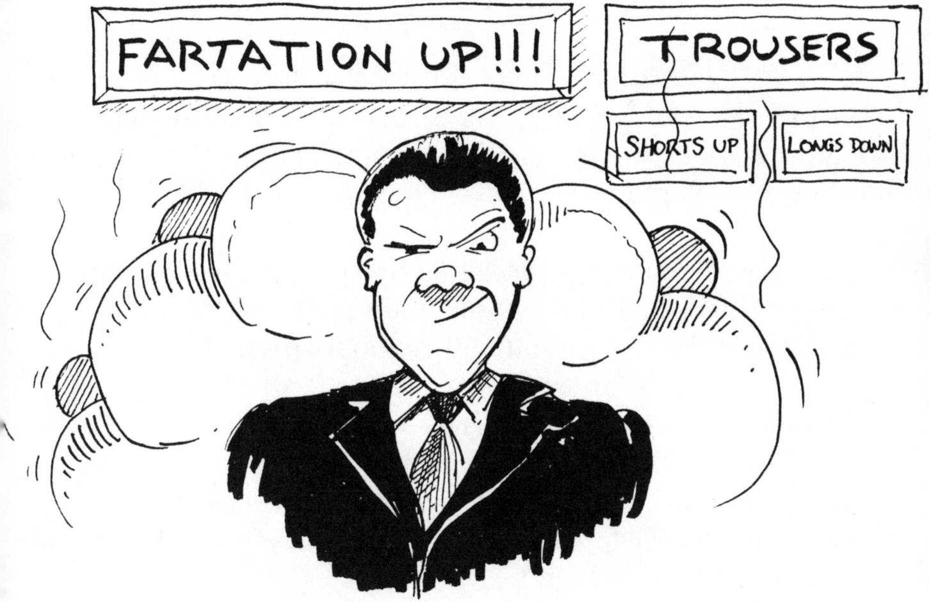
FARTATION UP!!!
TROUSERS
SHORTS UP
LONGS DOWN

WORLD WAFF II

Due to their deadly nature, farts have been used in warfare for thousands of years. Gas masks became part of everyone's life during the two World Wars as a defence against this most deadly of biological weapons.

The Allies used their bouncing-blap to destroy the German guff divisions in Europe and to bring the blitzfart to an end, despite the German's development of the 'doodle-parp'.

Churchill, who puffed on a cigar as a cover for his own slips, described this victory as "their finest humm", and was glad that no-one had to "fart them on the beaches". Had he read this paragraph, he might have said "This is the sort of guff up with which I will not put".

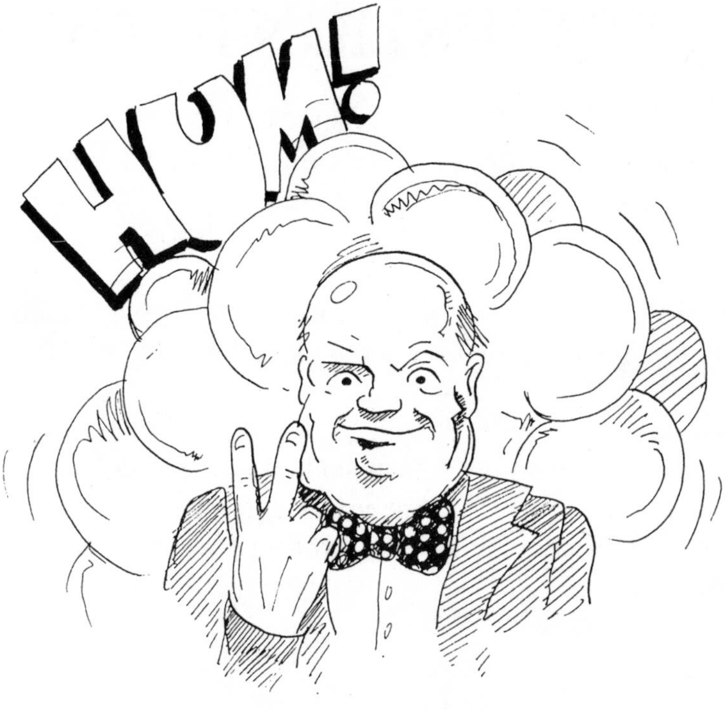

= COMBUSTION ENGINE =

Ever since Louis Pumpadour invented the intestinal combustion engine, to propel his farts on four wheels, mankind has been trying to fart faster and faster.

The first horseless chuffage, which was mass produced by Henry Fart in "any hue so long as it's blap", was painfully slow and did a good impression of a balloon being let down.

These days the Posh Parp 911 can reach an anal velocity of 168mph, and Formula 1 farts including the Italian Ferfarti get up to 300mph out of a chicane. Dragfartsters sometimes use a parachute to slow themselves down in case they reach terminal trumpocity.

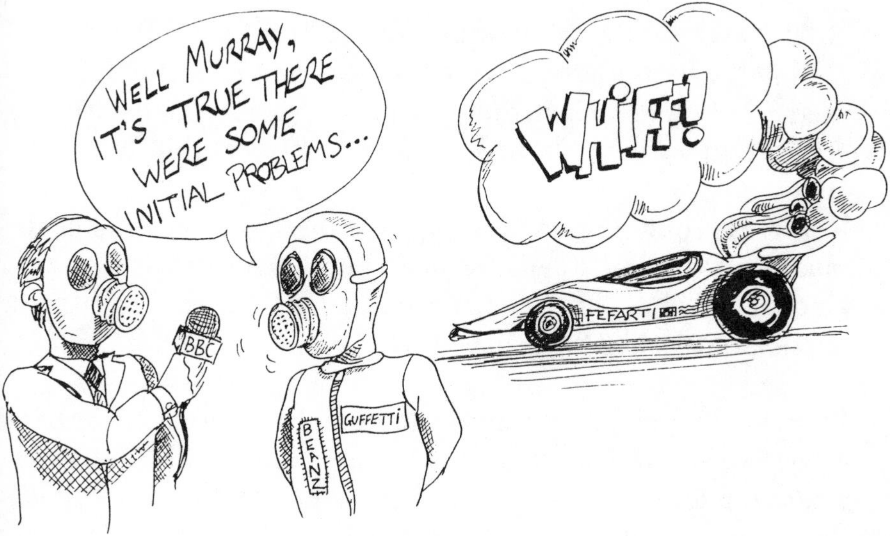
WELL MURRAY, IT'S TRUE THERE WERE SOME INITIAL PROBLEMS...
WHIFF!
BBC
GUFFETTI
BEANZ
FEFARTI

THE FINAL FARTIER

The search for the secret art of farting has now taken mankind out into the odourless vacuum of space. Solid booster guffs are used to lift spaceships from the planet, whilst small thrusters are used to position the vessels into the correct orbit.

Neil Fartstrong described his visit to the chuffy chappy in the moon as "One small guff for man, but a giant ripper for mankind", and ever since the boundaries of gufflessness have been relentlessly pushed back.

Perhaps the planet Youranus will hold the answer, or perhaps we will be saved by contact with extraterrestrial farts, but somewhere out there in the vast expanse of the Farty Way, there lies the secret to The Ancient Art of Farting...........